AGREEING
WITH
GOD

Declarations for Every Believer

Henry Sylvanus Altheide

WESTBOW
P R E S S
A DIVISION OF THOMAS NELSON

WestBow Press books may be ordered through
booksellers or by contacting:

WestBow Press
A Division of Thomas Nelson
1663 Liberty Drive
Bloomington, IN 47403
www.westbowpress.com
1-(866) 928-1240

ISBN: 978-1-4908-0407-1 (sc)
ISBN: 978-1-4908-0408-8 (e)

Library of Congress Control Number: 2013914229

Printed in the United States of America.

WestBow Press rev. date: 08/26/2013

To Vickie, Tim, Kristin and Anna.
Always remember that
the future is as bright as the promises of God.

Contents

Some Definitions to Consider

Sources for definitions, synonyms and antonyms:
1. Webster's New Universal Unabridged Dictionary
2. Merriam-Webster's Collegiate Dictionary, 11th Edition
3. The New American Roget's Thesaurus in Dictionary Form

Definitions for **AGREE** include: to have the same views, emotions, etc; harmonize in opinion or feeling; to give consent; assent; to live in concord or without contention; to come to one opinion or mind; to correspond; to be similar; conform; resemble. **Synonyms** include: coincide, concur, assent; see eye to eye. **Antonyms** include: refuse, decline, differ, disagree.

Definitions for **AFFIRM** include: to state or assert positively; maintain as true; *(e.g. He affirmed that all was well.)* to express agreement with or commitment to; uphold; support; to express dedication to *(e.g. affirm life)*. **Synonyms** include: avow, declare, insist, profess, protest, state, say, assure. **Antonyms** include: deny, gainsay.

Definitions for **AFFIRMATION** include: the act of affirming; something affirmed; the assertion that something exists or is true; a solemn declaration made under the penalties of perjury by a person who conscientiously declines taking an oath. **Synonyms** include: protestation, avowal, declaration, insistence, profession, statement. **Antonyms** include: disavowal, negation.

Definitions for **DECLARE** include: to make known or state clearly, especially in explicit and formal terms; to make evident: show; to state emphatically: affirm; *obsolete*: to make clear. **Synonyms** include: state, affirm, assert; protest; herald; proclaim; sound [used as a verb] *According to Webster's, to declare is to make known, sometimes in the face of actual or potential contradiction.* **Antonyms** include: deny, gainsay.

Definitions for **DECLARATION** include: the act of declaring: announcement; a positive, explicit or formal statement; something that is declared *(e.g. a declaration of love)*. **Synonyms** include: affirmation, avowal, insistence, protestation, profession, statement. **Antonyms** include: disavowal, denial.

Definitions for **CONFESS** include: to tell or make known; to own or admit as true; to acknowledge (sin) to God; to acknowledge one's belief or faith in; declare adherence to; to declare faith in or adherence to: profess. **Synonyms** include: admit, acknowledge, own, tell. **Antonyms** include: conceal, deny.

Definitions for **CONFESSION** include: something that is confessed; acknowledgement or disclosure; a formal statement of religious beliefs: creed. **Synonyms** include: admission, avowal, acknowledgement. **Antonyms** include disavowal, nonadmission.

Introduction

The words *affirmation* and *declaration* are used interchangeably in this book because of their closeness in meaning. A related word, *confession*, is often heard in Christian circles and Christianity itself has long been referred to as "the great confession". Today, as always, believers are encouraged to affirm, to declare and to confess the right things.

The purpose of this book is to inspire and encourage you. The simple declarations or affirmations you will find here are meant to serve as examples of how you can take God's Word very personally and affirm it in areas of your own life. I invite you to try out some of them for the next week, six months or fifty years. And by all means, paraphrase them if you wish, personalize them, make them your own. Whether you continue to use the ones written in this book, or make up your own as God inspires you, I believe you will become more aware of just how powerful your words are.

Upon reading this book for the first time, I would like to suggest that you read each chapter out loud. Quietly, yet audibly. Then, I encourage you to select just a few of the affirmations that are the most meaningful to you at this time. Take a few moments each morning to read your selections aloud, before you get busy with other things. Practice saying them with your eyes open, as well as closed. Repeat them several more times during the day and once again before you doze off to sleep. Every time you hear words of truth coming from your own lips, truth gets reinforced in your mind. Your thinking becomes more disciplined and you are uplifted as you hear yourself agreeing with God.

Some of the declarations contained in this little book are rather bold, and for this reason a few people feel awkward saying them out loud for the first time. Within a short while, however these same people often experience a heartfelt enthusiasm for life that boldly affirming the right stuff can bring. Some end up abandoning all shyness and shouting their confessions at the top of their lungs. If you happen to experience this same type of "heartburn", you may want to close all your windows or drive to a remote location!

As you read, you will notice a few prayers mixed in with the affirmations, and even a couple of commands. Praying and affirming work together in a believer's heart and often take place at the same time. Ecclesiastes 3:1-8 tells us that there is a time and place for everything in life. There is a time for affirmations, because our God chose to reveal Himself to us in words.[1] Affirming those words is always in season. There is certainly a time for prayer, because the Scriptures teach us to live prayerfully at all times,[2] conversing with our heavenly Father, to whom we have complete access, 24/7. And there are occasions in which commands are necessary, because Christians have been given power and authority which God expects us to use.[3]

After each declaration are a number of scripture references. Some of the references clearly document or support the affirmation. Others, however have been listed solely for your consideration because of information they contain.

I encourage you to look up each scripture listed for an affirmation that you choose. When doing so, please keep in mind that each verse of scripture should be studied within its context and in light of to whom it was originally written or spoken. Then, its relevance and application to our lives

---

1   Jeremiah 15:16; John 6:63; Matthew 4:4; Romans 1:16,17; 2 Peter 1:20-21

2   Luke 18:1; 1 Corinthians 14:15; Ephesians 2:18; 3:12; 6:18; 1 Thessalonians 5:17

3   John 14:12; Acts 1:8; 2:39; 1 Corinthians 12:1,7; Ephesians 1:19-23

today should be carefully considered and (where applicable) enthusiastically embraced.

The God and Father of our Lord Jesus Christ has given us so much to joyfully declare! May your relationship with Him deepen as you affirm and take action upon His promises.

 CHAPTER 1

God and His Word

The affirmations in this chapter have to do with the rightful place of God and His Word in our lives. When you come right down to it, getting to know our Creator is the most important thing any of us will accomplish in this life. Doing so will yield great benefits now, as well as in the future.

But what does knowing God really involve? When our human eyes behold the wonder of the stars, the oceans, or the human body, such examples of His handiwork clearly show His power and nature. As loudly as these may speak, however no one can truly know God without knowing His Word.

We must make an investment in the Bible, God's written revelation of Himself and His plans, if we want to build a genuine and vital relationship with Him. We learn from its pages that it's really all about relationship, not religion. And all successful relationships in our lives, whether with God or with people, require an investment of our time, our minds and our hearts.

SOME DECLARATIONS:

God made it all and God knows it all; I'm in good hands with God!

Genesis 1:1,27,31; Job 14:5; 42:2; Psalm 19:1; 33:5-6,13-15; 44:21; 95:3-6; 96:5; 103:14; 104:24; 139:1-4; 147:5; Proverbs 15:3; 22:4; Isaiah 33:6; 42:5; 49:15-16; Jeremiah 16:17; 23:24; John 1:3; Acts 1:24; 2:23; 5:29; 14:15; 15:18; 17:24; Romans 1:19; 16:25; Hebrews 4:13; 11:3; 13:5-6; 1 John 3:20

What do you see as you read these scriptures? Do any more Bible verses come to mind? Any new affirmations?

_____

_____

_____

_____

_____

GOD is the reason for everything! I am a part of His story and I am His child!

Genesis 1:1,27; Psalm 19:1; 31:15; 33:5-9; 103:17-19;
Ecclesiastes 12:13-14; Isaiah 43:7; John 1:3; Acts 14:15-17; Romans 1:19-20; 8:15-17; 10:9-13; 1 Corinthians 1:2-4,21,31; 8:3; 12:12-14; 15:28,57-58; 2 Corinthians 4:6; 6:18; Ephesians 1:4-5; 3:9-11; 1 Thessalonians 4:13-18; 2 Timothy 1:9; 1 John 3:1-2

_____

_____

_____

_____

_____

_____

God's words are in my heart and on my lips. They are life to me and health to my body.

Psalm 1:1-3; 12:6; 14:1; 19:7-11; 33:4; 107:20; 111:10; 112:1; 119:11,89,105; Proverbs 4:21-23; 16:24; 17:22; 22:4; Isaiah 40:8; 55:8-12; Jeremiah 15:16; Matthew 4:4; 7:19-20; Luke 4:4; John 14:27; 2 Corinthians 1:20; 10:5; Ephesians 3:17; Philippians 4:8; Colossians 3:16; Titus 3:8; Hebrews 4:12; James 1:21-25; 3:2-18; 1 Peter 2:24

_____

_____

_____

_____

_____

_____

My lips and my tongue are my friends today. They say what GOD wants them to say.

Psalm 19:4; 31:20; 34:1; Proverbs 4:24; 10:11; 12:14,18; 13:2-3; 14:3; 15:1-4; 16:23-24; 18:4,20-21; 21:23; Isaiah 55:8-12; Jeremiah 15:16; 2 Corinthians 4:13; Ephesians 4:25,29,31; Titus 3:8; Hebrews 10:23; 1 Peter 3:10

_____

_____

_____

_____

_____

_____

_____

The Word of MY God is full of power! It hits like a hammer and it burns like fire.

Genesis 1:3; Numbers 23:19; Psalm 14:1; 33:11; 89:34; 119:89; Isaiah 55:8-12; Jeremiah 23:29; 51:15-16; Romans 1:16; Ephesians 6:17; Colossians 2:2-3; 2 Timothy 3:16; Hebrews 4:12; 11:3; 1 Peter 2:24; James 1:21

_____

_____

_____

_____

_____

_____

I am not ashamed of the Good News of Jesus Christ! It saves! It delivers! It empowers!

Mark 8:38; Luke 9:26; John 1:12-17; 8:31-32; 10:10; Acts 1:8; 2:38-39; 4:19-20,33; 5:20,29; 10:38; Romans 1:16; 5:5; 10:9-13; 16:25; Galatians 1:4; Ephesians 3:1-9; 6:15,19-20; Philippians 1:14,20; 2 Timothy 1:8,12,16; 2:15; Hebrews 2:11; 7:25; 11:16; 1 Peter 2:24; 3:15-16; 4:16; 1 John 2:28

_____

_____

_____

_____

_____

_____

_____

_____

You have done so much for me! You have blessed my
life in so many ways! Thank-you for _____ and
_____ and _____. Praise You!

Deuteronomy 4:9; Psalm 4:8; 34:1-5; 40:1-2; 50:14; 68:19;
103:2; 105:1; 107:8,15,21,31; 127:3; Romans 8:32; 1Corinthians
1:30; 2:12; 12:13,18; 2 Corinthians 4:6; Galatians 1:4; 5:22-23;
Ephesians 1:3; 2:4-5; Colossians 1:12-14; 3:15; 2 Timothy 1:9;
Titus 3:3-7; 2 Peter 1:3-4

_____

_____

_____

_____

_____

_____

I'm God's child. He's my Father. He blesses me and
protects me.

Psalm 1:1-3; 4:8; 23:4; 31:20; 33:12; 46:1-11; 68:19; 91:1-16; 97:10;
112:1-3; 121:1-8; Proverbs 3:33-34; 22:4; 4:18; Matthew 6:31-33;
John 10:10,28; Romans 5:1-2,17; 8:31-32; 1 Corinthians 1:4-5;
2 Corinthians 9:8; Ephesians 1:4; 6:11; Colossians 1:12-13; James
1:25; 4:6-10; 2 Peter 1:3; 1 John 3:1; Hebrews 13:6

_____

_____

_____

_____

_____

_____

5

I call upon God and He delivers! (or) I call upon You and You deliver!

> Psalm 18:1-6; 20:1; 34:6-7,15; 40:1-2; 46:1,7,10; 50:15; 107:19-20,28; 121:2; 124:8; 138:7; 145:18; Mark 9:23; Romans 10:12; 2 Corinthians 1:3-10; Philippians 4:6; Colossians 1:13; Hebrews 4:16; James 4:6-7

_____

_____

_____

_____

_____

_____

_____

I wait upon You, Father God, with expectation... expecting Your favor today... expecting You to bless me because You say that You will, and You never lie.

> Numbers 23:19; Psalm 1:1-3; 25:1-5,14; 27:14; 34:15; 62:1,5; 68:19; 112:1-3,7-8; 119:90; Proverbs 22:4; Isaiah 40:31; Lamentations 3:22-25; Matthew 6:31-33; 21:22; Mark 9:23; John 14:21; 1 Corinthians 1:9; 2 Corinthians 9:8; Philippians 2:13; Titus 1:2; Hebrews 10:23; James 1:21-25; 4:6-7; 3 John 2

_____

_____

_____

_____

_____

_____

I'm Your child because You called me to be. I'm in Your presence right now and I know You're listening. You're never tired of me. You never give up on me. NEVER. You believe in me.

Numbers 23:19; Psalm 31:19-24; 33:18-21; 34:15; 40:1-4; 91:15-16; 103:10-11; Isaiah 40:28-31; Lamentations 3:22-23; Luke 18:1,7; Acts 2:39; Romans 8:15,32; 16:25; 1 Corinthians 1:9; 8:3; Ephesians 3:12; Colossians 1:12; 2 Timothy 1:9; Hebrews 4:16; 11:6; 1 Peter 5:6-7; 2 Peter 1:3; I John 1:9; 3:1-2

_____

_____

_____

_____

_____

I'm God's child and I matter to Him. I'm important to Him. He's never too busy to help ME. He WANTS to help me.

Psalm 25:14; 31:19; 34:15; 35:27; 40:1-4; 62:7-8; 103:13; 121:2; 124:8; 145:18; Isaiah 40:28-31; Matthew 7:11; Mark 9:23; Luke 15:4-32; Romans 2:11; 8:15,32; 10:12; 16:25; Ephesians 3:12,20; Philippians 2:13; Hebrews 4:16; 11:6; James 1:5-6; 4:6-7; 1 Peter 5:7

_____

_____

_____

_____

_____

_____

I am (state your full name) _____ and I belong to GOD. He loves me beyond my comprehension and He's on my side!

Psalm 40:1-4; 118:6; 138:3,8; 139:1-3; Proverbs 3:33-34; 4:18; Jeremiah 17:7-8; Luke 15:4-7; John 3:16; 10:28; 16:27; Romans 5:1-2,8; 8:31-39; 16:25; 1 Corinthians 6:20; 7:23; 8:3; Ephesians 2:4; 2 Thessalonians 2:16; 1 Peter 2:23; 1 John 3:1-2; 4:9

_____

_____

_____

_____

_____

_____

I am (state your full name) _____ and I'm a BELIEVER. I know my God and what He can do.

Genesis 1:1; Numbers 13:30; 23:19; Psalm 25:14; 33:17-19; 34:1-22; 35:27; Proverbs 3:33-34; Isaiah 26:3; 55:8-12; Jeremiah 9:23-24; Matthew 6:24-34; Luke 12:22-31; Acts 27:25; Romans 4:20-21; 10:12; 16:25; 2 Corinthians 9:8; Ephesians 1:19; 2:1,6; 3:20; Philippians 4:19; 2Timothy 1:12; Titus 3:4-7; Hebrews 11:6; 1John 1:5

_____

_____

_____

_____

_____

_____

I am (state your full name) _____ and I am a
BELIEVER. I believe the Word of God more than the word
of man.

> Numbers 23:19; Psalm 12:6; 89:34; 118:8-9; Isaiah 46:9-10; 55:8-
> 9; 66:1-2; Jeremiah 17:5-7; John 17:17; Acts 27:25; Romans 10:11;
> 2 Corinthians 1:21; Ephesians 1:19; 4:14; Titus 1:2; Hebrews 4:12;
> 11:6; James 1:17; 1 John 1:7

_____

_____

_____

_____

_____

_____

_____

_____

I don't care what the world says. I care what God says.

> Numbers 13:1,17-33; 14:1-24; 1 Samuel 16:7; Psalm 3:2-5; 12:6;
> 14:1; 111:10; 112:1,7-8; Proverbs 19:21; 22:4; Isaiah 66:1-2;
> Jeremiah 17:5-7; 51:17-19; John 8:44; 17:17; 1 Corinthians 1:18-25;
> 2 Corinthians 4:4; Ephesians 4:14; Colossians 2:8; 1Thessalonians
> 2:13; 4:15; Titus 1:2; Hebrews 4:12; 11:6; 1 John 1:16; 4:1

_____

_____

_____

_____

_____

_____

_____

_____

I am righteous and I am bold as a lion.

Joshua 1:9; Psalm 112:7; Proverbs 3:26; 14:26; 28:1; Acts 4:13,29,31; 9:29; 13:46; 14:3; 18:26; 19:8; 28:31; Romans 5:17-19; Ephesians 3:12; 6:10,19-20; Philippians 1:14,20; 1 Thessalonians 2:2; 1 Timothy 3:13; Hebrews 4:16; 10:19,35; 1 John 3:21; 4:4,17-18

_____

_____

_____

_____

_____

_____

_____

_____

GOD'S approval matters most to me. HE'S the One I'm living to please.

Proverbs 16:7; 18:12; 22:4; Ecclesiastes 12:13; Isaiah 66:1-2; John 12:43; 15:18; Acts 5:29; Romans 8:8; 1 Corinthians 1:20-31; 4:3-4; 6:19-20; 2 Corinthians 4:4; Ephesians 1:4; 2:10; Colossians 1:10; 1Thessalonians 4:1; 2 Timothy 2:1,15; Hebrews 11:6; 13:21; 1 John 3:22

_____

_____

_____

_____

_____

_____

_____

_____

My world view is simple: I agree with the One Who created it.

Genesis 1:1; Psalm 124:8; Proverbs 1:7-8,33; 2:1-6; 9:10; 15:14; 22:2; Ecclesiastes 12:13; John 3:16; 17:17; Acts 27:25; Romans 1:19-25; 1 Corinthians 1:18-25; 2 Corinthians 4:1-5,13,17-18; 5:18-20; 1 Timothy 2:1-5; James 3:16-18; 2 Peter 3:13-18; 1 John 5:19-20

_____

_____

_____

_____

_____

_____

_____

I know the meaning of life ... I'm living the meaning of life!

Psalm 16:11; 31:14-20; 36:6-9; 127:1-2; 128:1-4; Proverbs 1:7-8; 2:3-6; 3:13-18; 9:10; 11:28; 12:28; 14:26-27,34; 15:16; 19:23; 21:21; 22:2,4; Ecclesiastes 12:1,13; Jeremiah 9:23-24; 51:15-19; John 10:10; 17:3; Acts 4:9-12; 17:22-31; Romans 1:16-25; 6:6; Galatians 2:20; Ephesians 1:12; 5:8; 2Peter 1:2-4; 1John 1:1-4; 5:13

_____

_____

_____

_____

_____

_____

11

I don't have to live in constant crisis and suspense. My life is firm and stable because He is my stability.

Psalm 1:3; 36:7-8; 37:1-7,16-19,25,39-40; 46:1-3; 61:3-4; 128:1-4; Proverbs 1:33; 2:8; 11:28; Isaiah 26:3-4; 33:6; Jeremiah 17:5-8; Malachi 3:6,10-11; Luke 6:47-49; Romans 8:31-32; 1 Corinthians 3:10-11; 10:13; Ephesians 6:10-11,18; Philippians 4:1-8; James 1:2-8; 1 Peter 5:5-10

_____

_____

_____

_____

_____

_____

Life is meaningless without You and I am nothing without You. I NEED YOU.

Psalm 14:1; 108:12-13; 127:1-2; Proverbs 1:7-8; 2:1-6; 9:10; 11:28; 15:16; Ecclesiastes 12:13; Isaiah 44:6-20; 50:10-11; Jeremiah 9:23-24; 17:5-14; John 10:10; 15:5-8; Romans 1:19-25; 1Corinthians 1:18-31; 15:10,58; Galatians 2:20; Ephesians 2:1-5; 2 Peter 1:2-8; 3:13-18; 1 John 5:12

_____

_____

_____

_____

_____

_____

_____

I live in the realm of the supernatural, for I was fathered by a supernatural God. I belong to Him and I serve Him. I will not limit Him, for He is Who He is!

Genesis 1:1; Numbers 23:19; Psalm 19:1; 90:2; 95:3; 102:25-27; 107:29; Proverbs 15:3; Isaiah 40:28-31; 46:9; 55:8-9; 57:15; 66:1-2; Jeremiah 32:17; Daniel 11:32; Matthew 9:8; Mark 9:23; Luke 1:37; John 10:29; 14:12,21,23; Romans 4:17; 6:4; 1 Corinthians 1:27-29; 12:1,7; Ephesians 2:6,10; 3:20; 6:10-12; Colossians 1:27; Hebrews 11:3,6; Revelation 21:1

_____

_____

_____

_____

_____

_____

I was made to walk with God. I CAN walk with Him. I can walk in His power.

Psalm 1:1-3; 25:14; Proverbs 4:18; Isaiah 40:28-31; 43:7; Mark 9:23; John 14:12,21,23; Acts 1:8; 2:39; Romans 5:1-2; 6:4,11; 10:12; 1 Corinthians 6:19-20; 12:7; 2 Corinthians 3:6; 5:7; Ephesians 1:17-19; 2:10; 3:20; 6:10-17; Philippians 4:13; Colossians 1:12-13; 1Timothy 1:9; Hebrews 11:6; 2 Peter 1:3-4; 1 John 1:7

_____

_____

_____

_____

_____

_____

_____

YOU called me to Your Word. Teach me, Father. I need Your help to understand who I now am!

John 14:12,21; Romans 5:1-2; 6:3-11; 8:1-4; 12:2-3; 16:25; 1 Corinthians 1:30; 6:19,20; 12:1; 2 Corinthians 1:21; 3:18; 5:17; Galatians 5:1; Ephesians 1:17-19; 2:6,10; 4:15,22-24; 6:10; Philippians 1:6; 2:13; 3:9; Colossians 1:10,27-28; 2:7,10; 3:9-11; Hebrews 13:20-21; James 1:18; 2Peter 1:2-8

_____

_____

_____

_____

_____

_____

_____

Open my eyes, Father. Show me who I am in Christ!

John 14:12,21; Romans 5:1-2; 6:3-11; 8:1-4; 12:2-3; 16:25; 1 Corinthians 1:30; 6:19-20; 12:1; 2 Corinthians 1:21; 3:18; 5:17; Galatians 5:1; Ephesians 1:17-19; 2:6,10; 4:15,22-24; 6:10; Philippians 3:9; Colossians 1:10,27-28; 2:6-7,10; 3:3,9-11; 2 Peter 1:2-8; Hebrews 13:21; Jude 20-21

_____

_____

_____

_____

_____

_____

_____

I choose to be authentic, to put off the old man and put on the new.

Romans 6:3-11; 7:22-25; 8:6-8,13; 12:2-3,16-17; 13:13-14; 1Corinthians 2:8,12; 6:19-20; 13:1-7; 2Corinthians 2:14-15; 5:17; 8:21; Galatians 5:22-26; Ephesians 2:10; 4:22-24; Philippians 1:9; Colossians 1:27; 2:6; 3:3,9-11; 1Thessalonians 4:12; Titus 3:5; James 1:21-22; 2 Peter 1:2-8; Jude 20-21

_____

_____

_____

_____

_____

_____

_____

_____

_____

_____

_____

_____

_____

_____

_____

_____

_____

_____

CHAPTER 2

Healthy Minds

Where do each of us spend a great deal of our time? Right between our own ears, of course! Yes, the mind is where much of our lives takes place. It is where we process all the messages we receive and where we determine how we'll respond to them.

Here's some good news: <u>we</u> can choose, intentionally and deliberately, what we will think about each and every moment. Where do we want to live, mentally? By choosing the right thoughts our minds can be Home, Sweet Home, rather than Heartbreak Hotel; a haven, rather than a hurricane.

The Bible has much to say regarding our thoughts and God's desire for us to be transformed by the voluntary renewing of our minds. The godly affirmations you find in this chapter will help you today as you move forward on your personal journey with our heavenly Father. With Him leading, it is a well-lit journey, filled with discovery, transformation and love.

SOME DECLARATIONS:

Today is (state the day of the week, then the full date) _____ and I'm still here! I'm ____ years old, I'm ALIVE, I'm THANKFUL and I'm EXCITED!

Psalm 16:11; 25:14; 40:3; 70:4; 100:1-5; 104:33-34; 105:3-4; 118:24,28; Proverbs 3:2,5-6; 4:18; Ecclesiastes 9:9-10; 12:13; Romans 6:3-4; 15:13; 2 Corinthians 9:15; Ephesians 5:19-20; Philippians 4:4; Colossians 1:12; 2:7; 3:15; 1Thessalonians 5:16-18; 1 Peter 1:8; 1 John 1:4; 5:11

What do you see as you read these scriptures? Do any more Bible verses come to mind? Any new affirmations?

_____

_____

_____

_____

_____

Good morning, Father! Thanks for letting me live today. Thanks for letting me know YOU. Thanks for what I get to do today. Thanks for the chance to love.

Psalm 25:14; 104:33-34; 105:3-4; Proverbs 3:6,27; Ecclesiastes 9:9-10; 12:13; Jeremiah 9:23-24; John 15:12-13; 17:3; 1 Corinthians 16:14; Galatians 6:2; Ephesians 4:15; 5:2,20-21; Philippians 4:4; Colossians 1:12; 3:14-15,17; 1 Peter 1:22-24; 1 John 3:11-19

_____

_____

_____

_____

_____

_____

Jesus is the Lord of my life. I walk like he walked. I think like he thought. I'm in love with my Father and I'm at perfect peace.

Isaiah 26:3; Matthew 22:37; Mark 12:30; Luke 10:27; John 8:6; 14:12,31; 15:1-5; Acts 10:38; Romans 1:3; 5:1; 10:9-13; 1 Corinthians 1:2; 2 Corinthians 10:5; Galatians 5:22-23; Ephesians 4:5; 5:2; 6:24; Philippians 2:5; Colossians 2:6; 3:13,15,17,24; 1 Peter 2:21; 2 Peter 1:8; 1 John 2:6,28; 5:3

_____

_____

_____

_____

_____

_____

My name is _____. Jesus is my Lord and Savior and I am forgiven! I'm free from sin and I'm free from guilt. I'm dead to sin and I'm alive unto righteousness.

Psalm 103:3,12; John 8:36; Acts 26:18; Romans 5:1; 6:3-13; 8:1; 10:4,9-10; 13:12-14; 1 Corinthians 1:2,30; 2 Corinthians 5:21; Ephesians 1:7; 4:24,32; Galatians 1:4; 2:20; Philippians 3:9; Colossians 1:14; 1:21-23; 2:13; 3:3,13; Titus 3:3-7; 1 John 1:7,9; 2:2,12; 5:12

_____

_____

_____

_____

_____

_____

My old nature was crucified with Christ. I'm dead to sin. I'm alive to God!

Romans 1:16-17; 3:21-26; 4:25; 5:1,8-11; 6:1-18; 8:1-13; 10:9-10; 13:12-14; 1 Corinthians 1:2,30; 2 Corinthians 5:17-21; Galatians 2:20; Ephesians 1:4; 2:1-5; 4:22-24; Philippians 2:5; 3:9-10; Colossians 1:13-14; 1:21-23; 2:13; 3:3,9-10; Titus 3:3-7; 1 Peter 2:24; 1 John 1:7,9; 2:2,12

_____

_____

_____

_____

_____

I love "me", because God loves me! He loves me right NOW!

Psalm 31:20-21; 103:13; 104:34; 105:3-4; Jeremiah 31:3; John 3:16; 14:21; 16:27; Romans 5:8; 8:35-39; Ephesians 2:4; 2 Thessalonians 2:16; Titus 3:4-6; Hebrews 12:6; 1 Peter 5:7; 1 John 3:1; 4:8-19

_____

_____

_____

_____

_____

_____

_____

I am valuable because of who I AM, not because of what I DO. I am God's child and I am valuable!

Luke 15:11-24; Acts 20:28; Romans 3:20-24; 5:17-19; 8:15-17; 1 Corinthians 1:2-4; 1:26-31; 12:13-27; Galatians 2:16; 4:6; 5:1; Ephesians 1:2-6,23; 2:8-10; 3:12; Colossians 1:12-13; 2 Timothy 1:9; Titus 3:4-7; 1 John 3:1-2; 5:12

_____

_____

_____

_____

_____

_____

_____

I'm living in grace and I'm living in love; I'm keeping my thoughts on things above!

Psalm 104:33-34; 119:165; John 16:12-13; Acts 20:32; Romans 3:24; 5:2,15,17,20-21; 12:2-3,9-10; 1 Corinthians 15:10; 2 Corinthians 4:18; 6:1; Galatians 1:6; 2:21; Ephesians 1:2,4,6-7,17-18; 2:5,7,8; 4:2,7,15,23,29; Philippians 2:2-5; 4:8; Colossians 2:2; 3:1-2,16; 4:6; 1 Thessalonians 1:3,10; 3:12 2 Timothy 1:9; 2:1; Hebrews 4:16; 12:1-3; 1 Peter 3:7; 4:10; 5:5; 2 Peter 3:18; 1 John 3:18; 5:21

_____

_____

_____

_____

_____

_____

_____

I choose to plant GOOD things in my heart and I will HARVEST good things!

Psalm 1:1-3; 19:10-11; 105:3-4; 112:1-3; 119:11; Proverbs 15:13,15; 18:20-21; 22:4; Jeremiah 15:16; Matthew 4:4; 7:19-22; 12:35; Mark 9:23; Luke 4:4; Galatians 6:7-9; 2 Corinthians 10:5; Philippians 4:6-9; Colossians 3:12; Hebrews 10:23; James 1:21-25; 2 Peter 1:2-8

I cannot transform myself, Father... You know the person I can really be and only YOU can transform me... so I'll keep doing my job and I know that You'll do Yours.

1 Samuel 16:7; Psalm 16:7; 73:26; Matthew 3:11-12; John 3:6-7; 6:28-29,63; 15:1-5; 16:13-15; Romans 6:4; 7:18; 8:29; 12:2; 13:12-14; 16:25; 1 Corinthians 3:6-7; 14:12; 15:58; 2Corinthians 3:18; Galatians 5:16-23; Ephesians 1:17-19; 2:10; 4:22-24; Philippians 1:6,9; 2:12-13; 3:13-14; 4:1; Colossians 3:1-3,16; 1:27; 3:1-3,10-11; 2Thessalonians 3:5; Hebrews 12:6-11; 2 Peter 1:4-8; Jude 20-21

God is the strength of my life! God is my joy!

Nehemiah 8:10; Psalm 16:11; 18:1; 23:1-6; 25:14; 27:5,14; 31:20-21,24; 27:1; 61:3; 62:7; 71:16; 94:17-19; 104:34; 119:165; Isaiah 40:31; 55:12; Jeremiah 9:23-24; 15:16; Romans 5:11; 15:13; Galatians 5:22; Ephesians 6:10; Philippians 4:4; 2 Timothy 2:1; 1 Peter 5:10; 1 John 1:4

_____

_____

_____

_____

_____

_____

_____

_____

God refreshes me and restores my soul!

Psalm 23:3; 27:14; 31:24; 34:2,22; 62:1,5; 63:1-5; 94:17-19; 103:5; 105:4; 107:9; 138:3; 147:3; Proverbs 16:24; 25:25; Isaiah 40:29-31; 57:15; 58:11; Colossians 3:15; Hebrews 4:11; 6:18-19; 12:1-3; James 1:21; 3 John 2

_____

_____

_____

_____

_____

_____

_____

_____

I will live today without fear... I'm not afraid of anyONE or anyTHING, and I'm not afraid of the future.

Deuteronomy 7:18; Joshua 1:9; Psalm 4:8; 23:4; 27:1,5,14; 31:15,20,21; 34:4; 46:2,10; 56:3; 91:5; 112:7-8; 119:165; Proverbs 3:5-6,24-25; 4:18; 14:26-27; 29:25; Jeremiah 1:8; Ezekiel 2:6; Matthew 6:34; John 14:1-3,27; Ephesians 6:10; Philippians 1:14; 2 Timothy 1:7; Hebrews 2:14-15; 13:6; 1 Peter 3:14; 1 John 4:4,18; Jude 20-21

_____

_____

_____

_____

_____

_____

The peace of God rules my heart and I refuse to worry about anything.

Psalm 4:8; 31:24; 37:1,7-8,37; 112:7; 119:165; Proverbs 16:3; 24:19; Isaiah 9:6; 26:3; Jeremiah 17:7-8; Matthew 6:25-34; 10:19; Mark 13:11; Luke 12:22-31; John 14:27; Romans 12:18; 1 Corinthians 14:33; 2 Corinthians 13:11; Ephesians 2:14; Philippians 4:6-9; Colossians 3:15; Hebrews 13:6; James 3:17,18; 1 Peter 5:7

_____

_____

_____

_____

_____

_____

_____

_____

Anxiety and fear will not control ME; I choose to be peaceful. I choose the peace of God.

Psalm 4:8; 23:4; 25:14; 27:5; 31:20,24; 37:7; 46:10; 62:8; 91:1-16; 112:7; 119:165; Proverbs 16:3; 24:19; Isaiah 9:6; 26:3; Jeremiah 17:7-8; Matthew 6:25-34; Mark 13:11; John 14:27; Romans 12:18; 15:13; 2 Corinthians 10:5; 13:11; Ephesians 2:14; Philippians 4:6-7; Colossians 3:15; 1 Peter 5:7; 1 John 4:4

_____

_____

_____

_____

_____

_____

_____

I choose to be happy. I choose a merry heart.

1 Chronicles 16:27; 2 Chronicles 7:10; Psalm 9:2; 16:9; 31:24; 32:11; 34:2; 40:16; 64:10; 67:4; 68:3; 70:4; 100:2; 104:34; 105:43; 118:24; 122:1; 127:5; 128:2; 144:15; 146:5; Proverbs 3:13,18; 12:25; 14:21; 15:13,15,30; 16:20; 17:22; Ecclesiastes 9:7; Isaiah 25:9; Joel 2:21; Luke 15:32; Acts 2:46; 14:17; Romans 14:22; 15:13; Philippians 4:4,8; 1 Timothy 6:6; James 5:13; 1 Peter 3:14; 1 John 1:4

_____

_____

_____

_____

_____

_____

_____

Perfect love kicks out my fear... love makes me fearless...
I'm fearless because I love!

Matthew 14:27-31; 22:37-39; Mark 12:30-31; Luke 6:35; 10:27-37; John 15:12-13,17; 18:4-8; 19:10-11; Acts 5:29; 28:3-5,31; Romans 12:9-10; 1 Corinthians 13:7; Ephesians 5:1-2; 2 Timothy 1:7; Hebrews 13:6; 1 Peter 3:14-15; 4:8; 1 John 3:11-17; 4:16-21; 5:2-5; Jude 21

_____

_____

_____

_____

_____

God is at work in my life! I refuse to be discouraged. I choose to be confident. I AM CONFIDENT.

Joshua 1:9; 1 Samuel 30:6; Job 42:11-17; Psalm 25:14; 27:5,14; 31:24; 37:4-5,34; 39:1-11; 62:7,8; 118:6-9; Proverbs 3:26; 14:26; 17:22; Isaiah 26:3; 40:31; 41:10; Jeremiah 29:11-13; John 14:27; Romans 15:13; 1 Corinthians 10:13;13:7; 15:58; 16:13; 2 Corinthians 4:1,16-18; Galatians 6:9; Ephesians 3:12; 6:10; Philippians 1:6; 2:13; 4:13; 2 Thessalonians 3:13; Hebrews 10:35; 12:1-3; James 1:2-6; 1 John 5:14; Jude 20-21

_____

_____

_____

_____

_____

_____

_____

God is alive in me and I'm walking with Him... I am absolutely walking with HIM.

Psalm 25:12-14; 31:20-24; 104:33-34; Romans 8:9-10,15; 2 Corinthians 4:7; Ephesians 1:23; 2:22; 5:1,8; Colossians 1:27; 1Timothy 4:8,15-16; 5:6,11-12; 2 Timothy 1:9,12; 2:19-22; Titus 3:5-8; Hebrews 4:2,16; 10:23; 12:1; 13:6-7; 1 Peter 2:9-10; 3:15; 4:10-11; 5:6-7; 2 Peter 1:3-4,10; 1 John 1:7; 2:6; 4:4,12; 5:11-14; Jude 20-21

_____

_____

_____

_____

_____

_____

_____

You have forgiven me and I forgive myself. It's a new day!

2 Chronicles 7:14; Psalm 40:3; 103:3,12; Proverbs 24:16; Isaiah 1:2-4,18-19; Jeremiah 33:3-8; Joel 2:12-13,25; Romans 6:4; 16:25; Ephesians 1:7; 4:32; Philippians 3:13; Colossians 1:14; 2:13; 3:13; Matthew 6:12,14-15; 1 John 1:9; 3:20-21

_____

_____

_____

_____

_____

_____

_____

I am so happy to be alive today! I LOVE MY LIFE! God has blessed me so incredibly!

Psalm 4:8; 31:15,19-21; 68:19; 100:4; 103:2-5; 104:33,34; 118:24; 128:1-4; Proverbs 10:22; 15:15-17; 17:1,22; Matthew 6:33; John 3:16; 10:10; Romans 15:6-7,13; 1 Corinthians 2:12; 2 Corinthians 1:22; 4:6; 8:9; 9:15; Galatians 3:14; Ephesians 1:3-4; Philippians 4:4,8; Colossians 1:12-13,21-22; 1Thessalonians 5:16-18; 1 Timothy 6:17; 2 Timothy 1:9; Titus 3:4-7; Hebrews 2:15; James 1:5,17; 2 Peter 1:3; 1 John 1:4

_____

_____

_____

_____

_____

_____

(say to your problem) You are nothing, compared to GOD!

Genesis 1:1-31; 39:21-23; 45:6-10; Exodus 14:9-31; Numbers 13:30; 14:6-9; Joshua 1:3-9; 24:15-17; 1 Samuel 17:32-50; 2 Kings 6:15-18; Psalm 4:8; 27:1,5; 31:19-24; 62:7; 118:6-9; Proverbs 30:5; Isaiah 40:12-31; 55:10-11; Jeremiah 29:11-14; 33:3-9; Daniel 3:12-28; Luke 1:37-38; 17:19-20; Romans 1:20; 8:28,31-39; Ephesians 3:20; 1 Corinthians 1:25; 2 Corinthians 1:3-4,8-10; James 1:2; 1 John 4:4

_____

_____

_____

_____

_____

_____

(say to your fear) SHUT UP!... Get out of the way... God & I are coming through!

> Numbers 13:30; Deuteronomy 7:18; Joshua 1:9; 1 Samuel 17:26,37,45-51; Psalm 4:8; 23:4; 27:1,5,14; 31:24; 46:2,10; Isaiah 41:10; Jeremiah 1:8; Ezekiel 2:6; Daniel 3:16-18; Matthew 14:29-30; John 14:27; Romans 8:31-39; 2 Corinthians 1:10; Ephesians 6:10; 2 Timothy 1:7; Hebrews 13:6; 1 John 4:4,17-18

_____

_____

_____

_____

_____

(say to the devil) SHUT UP! You no longer own me, nor have any power over me. Christ redeemed me and I'M A FREE MAN/WOMAN. You're a liar and you're an absolute loser! I'M a WINNER... now, and for all eternity!

> Isaiah 14:12-17; John 8:36,44; Acts 20:28; Romans 3:24; 8:37; 16:20; 1 Corinthians 6:20, 7:23; 10:13; 2Corinthians 2:14; Galatians 3:13; 4:4-5; Ephesians 1:7,18-23; Colossians 1:13-14; Titus 2:14; Hebrews 9:12; James 1:2,12-13; 1Peter 1:18-19; 1John 4:4; 5:4; Revelation 20:10

Note: As the Scriptures do not tell us to carry on conversations with God's archenemy, I am not advocating that anyone make a practice of it. Under certain conditions, however, affirmations such as the ones above have helped believers get through difficult times, boldly.

_____

_____

_____

_____

_____

Jesus could return TODAY. This could be my last day here. What kind of person do I want to be today?

Psalm 34:1; 118:24; John 14:12; Acts 1:8,11; 10:38; Romans 1:16; 13:12-14; 15:13; 1 Corinthians 12:7; 13:1-7; 14:12; 15:58; 2Corinthians 5:9,20; Ephesians 4:1,24; 5:1-2; 6:10; Philippians 2:5; 3:1,14; Colossians 3:23; 1 Timothy 6:19; 2 Timothy 2:1; 4:2,8; Hebrews 12:1; James 1:12; 1 Peter 1:22; 1 John 2:28; 3:3; 5:21; Jude 20-21

_____

_____

_____

_____

_____

I have eternal life... WOW!... I HAVE ETERNAL LIFE!!!

John 3:16; 6:63,68; 14:2; 17:2-3; Romans 5:21; 6:23; 15:13; 1 Corinthians 15:19,49,58; 2 Corinthians 4:18; 5:1; Ephesians 1:18; Philippians 3:20-21; Colossians 1:5; 3:4; 1 Thessalonians 1:10; 4:13-18; 5:9-10; 2 Thessalonians 2:1-3,13-17; 3:5; 2 Timothy 1:9-10; Titus 1:2; 3:7; Hebrews 5:9; 6:18-20; 9:28; 1 Peter 1:3-4,13,23-25; 3:15; 5:10; 2 Peter 1:10-11; 1 John 2:17,25,28; 3:2-3; 5:11-13

_____

_____

_____

_____

_____

_____

CHAPTER 3

Healthy Bodies

People today are frequently bombarded with messages inviting them to take one product for depression, another product for this disease and still another for that disease. There seems to be no shortage of physical ailments and chemicals to treat them. Without a doubt, some of man's medications can be helpful and we have all benefited from them at one time or another.

This chapter invites you to begin incorporating God's medicine into your life as well, by confessing with your lips some of the truths He has revealed regarding health and healing. Though extremely costly, our healing, just as our salvation, was paid for long ago by God's Son when he willingly laid down his life for us. With all that we have in Christ, it is now our privilege to speak healing words to ourselves and to others, with God given authority.

My name is _____ and Jesus is the Lord of my life. Sickness and disease have no power over me because Jesus became a curse on my behalf! He fulfilled the Old Testament Law's demands and redeemed me from its curse.

Deuteronomy 28:15-68; Isaiah 53:3-5; Matthew 4:23; 9:22; 10:8; John 8:36; Acts 3:6,16; 9:34; 10:38; Romans 7:4; 8:3-4; 10:4,9-12; Galatians 3:13,24-25; 4:4-5; Ephesians 3:20; Colossians 2:14; 1 Peter 1:18-19; 2:24

What do you see as you read these scriptures? Do any more Bible verses come to mind? Any new affirmations?

_____

_____

_____

_____

Christ redeemed me from everything in the curse of the Old Testament Law, including sickness, disease and poverty.

Deuteronomy 28:15-68; Isaiah 53:3-5; Matthew 4:23; 9:22; 10:8; John 8:36; Acts 3:6,16; 9:34; 10:38; Romans 7:4; 8:3-4; 10:4; Galatians 3:13; 4:4-5; Ephesians 3:20; Colossians 2:14; 1 Peter 1:18-19; 2:24

_____

_____

_____

_____

I will not allow any of the curses of the Old Testament Law to come on my body. CHRIST is my Big "C", not cancer!

Deuteronomy 28:15-68; Isaiah 53:3-5; Matthew 4:23; 8:17; 9:22,28-29; 11:5; Luke 6:17-19; John 8:36; Acts 3:6,16; 4:9-12; 9:34; 10:38; Romans 10:4; 1 Corinthians 1:30; 5:7; Galatians 2:20; 3:13; 4:4-7; 6:14; Ephesians 1:18-23; 2:20-22; Philippians 2:9-10; Colossians 1:27; 1 Peter 1:18-19; 2:24

_____

_____

_____

_____

_____

_____

_____

By the wounds of my Savior my _____ was/were healed.

Exodus 12:3,6-8,11; Psalm 105:37; Isaiah 53:3-5; Matthew 8:17; 10:8; 26:67; 27:26-35; Mark 14:65; 15:15-20,24-25; Luke 22:63-64; 23:33; Acts 3:6,16; 5:15-16; 9:34; 10:38; 14:8-10; 28:8-9; 1 Corinthians 5:7; 10:16; 11:23-30; Galatians 3:13; 1 Peter 1:18-19; 2:24

_____

_____

_____

_____

_____

_____

_____

_____

I speak peace to the turbulence in my body, just as Jesus spoke peace to the turbulence of the sea. I call my body HEALED. I declare it in his name.

Psalm 103:2-3; 107:2,20; Proverbs 10:11; 12:14,18; 13:3; 14:3; 15:2,4; 16:23-24; Isaiah 53:3-5; Matthew 8:5-13,23-26; 9:22,28-29; 10:8; 18:18; Mark 11:23, 24; John 14:12; Acts 3:6,16; 9:34; 10:38; 14:8-10; 28:8-9; Ephesians 1:20-23; 3:20; 1 Peter 2:24

_____

_____

_____

_____

_____

(speak calmly and confidently to your symptoms) You can't have me. You have no right to live in my body. You will leave, in the name of Jesus Christ. I call myself healed.

Exodus 15:26; Psalm 107:2,20; Proverbs 10:11; 12:14,18; 13:3; 14:3; 15:2,4; 16:23-24; Isaiah 53:3-5; Matthew 4:23; 8:5-13; 9:22,28-29; 10:8; Mark 11:23-24; John 14:12; Acts 3:6,16; 5:15-16; 9:34; 10:38; 14:8-10; 28:8-9; Ephesians 1:20-23; 3:20; 1 Peter 2:24

_____

_____

_____

_____

_____

Note: The Lord Jesus Christ made known the Father and always did the will of the Father. The Scriptures inform us that when multitudes of people came to Jesus for healing, he never refused anyone, for any reason whatsoever, nor did he suggest at any time to any individual that sickness was God's will for them. If God directs you to ask another believer to minister healing to you, then do it with absolute confidence, knowing that it is absolutely God's will for you to be healed and that you as His child are worthy of receiving it.

Jesus took away my sickness and carried my disease. Sickness, I refuse to allow you to control and dominate me. You are NO match for the power of God's Word. God's Word lives in me richly and brings healing to every fiber of my being.

Psalm 103:2-3; 107:20; 112:7; Isaiah 53:3-5; Matthew 8:17; 8:5-13; 9:22,28-29; 10:8; Luke 4:40; John 6:63; 8:31-32,36; 14:12; Acts 3:6,16; 9:34; 5:12-16; 10:38; 14:8-10; 28:8-9; Romans 1:16; Galatians 2:20; 3:13; 4:4-5; Ephesians 1:20-23; 3:20; Colossians 3:16; 1 Peter 2:24

_____

_____

_____

_____

_____

GOD'S words are in my heart and on my lips. They are life to me and health to my body.

Psalm 1:1-3; 12:6; 14:1; 19:7-11; 33:4; 103:2-3; 107:20; 111:10; 112:1; 119:11,89,105; Proverbs 4:21-23; 16:24; 17:22; 22:4; Isaiah 40:8; 55:8-12; Jeremiah 15:16; Matthew 4:4; 7:19-20; Luke 4:4; John 14:27; 2 Corinthians 1:20; 10:5; Ephesians 3:17; Philippians 4:8; Colossians 3:16; Titus 3:8; Hebrews 4:12; James 1:21-25; 3:2-18; 1Peter 2:24

_____

_____

_____

_____

_____

_____

God is my physician! The Word of God is my medicine!

Exodus 15:26; Psalm 30:2; 103:2-3; 107:2,20; Proverbs 4:20-22;
Isaiah 53:3-5; Malachi 3:6; Matthew 4:23; 8:5-13; 9:22,28-29;
10:8; 11:5; Mark 8:22-26; Luke 6:17-19; 18:35-43; John 14:12;
Acts 3:1-8,16; 5:12-16; 14:8-10; 28:8-9; Ephesians 1:20-23; 3:20;
1 Peter 2:24

_____

_____

_____

_____

_____

_____

_____

I will not die, but I will LIVE and I will declare the works of my God!

Exodus 15:26; Psalm 73:28; 103:2-3; 107:2,20-21; 118:17; 119:49-
50; Proverbs 18:21; Isaiah 25:1,4; 53:3-5; Matthew 4:23; 8:5-13;
9:22,28-29; 10:8; Luke 18:35-43; Acts 3:6-8,16; 4:9-10; 5:16; 9:34;
14:20; 28:8-9; Galatians 2:20

_____

_____

_____

_____

_____

_____

_____

I believe and therefore I speak... I honor You by taking YOUR medicine.

Exodus 15:26; Psalm 91:14-16; 103:2-3; 107:20; Proverbs 4:20-22; 13:3; 16:23-24; Isaiah 53:3-5; Matthew 4:23; 8:5-13; 10:8; 12:34-35; John 14:12; 2 Corinthians 4:13; Ephesians 1:20-23; 3:20; Hebrews 11:6; 1 Peter 2:24

_____

_____

_____

_____

_____

_____

_____

Father God, I now minister Your Word of truth to my body. Let it now flow through my blood stream. Let it flow to every cell of my body, restoring and transforming me. Thank-you for sending Your Word to heal ME. Praise You!

Exodus 15:26; Psalm 103:2-3; 107:20; 139:14; Proverbs 16:23-24; Isaiah 53:3-5; Matthew 4:23; 8:5-13; 9:22; 10:8; Luke 18:35-43; John 8:31-32; 14:12; Acts 3:1-8; 3:16; 5:12-16; 9:40-41; 14:8-10; 28:8-9; Romans 8:32; 2 Corinthians 1:20; Galatians 2:20; Ephesians 1:20-23; 3:20; Hebrews 4:12; 11:6; 1 Peter 2:24

_____

_____

_____

_____

_____

_____

_____

God lives in MY body through His gift of holy spirit that He gave me. (Speak to your body) Body, I demand that you release the proper chemicals and that you be in perfect chemical balance.

Psalm 103:2-3; 139:14; Isaiah 53:3-5; Matthew 4:23; 8:5-13; 9:22; 10:8; John 14:12; Acts 1:8; 2:38-39; 3:6; 5:12-16; 9:34,40; 14:8-10; 1 Corinthians 6:19-20; Galatians 2:20; Ephesians 1:20-23; 2:22; 3:20; Colossians 1:27; 1Peter 2:24

_____

_____

_____

_____

_____

_____

I demand that my blood cells destroy every disease germ that tries to live inside of me. Cells, I say to you in the name of Jesus Christ: BE NORMAL. BE WELL.

Isaiah 53:3-5; Matthew 4:23; 8:5-13; 9:22,28-29; 10:8; Mark 11:23, 24; Luke 17:6; John 14:12; Acts 3:6,16; 5:12-16; 9:34; 14:8-10; 28:8-9; Galatians 3:13; Ephesians 1:19-23; 2:22; 3:20; Colossians 1:27; 1Peter 2:24

_____

_____

_____

_____

_____

_____

Every beat of my heart is healthy and strong... every beat cleanses me of disease and pain.

> Exodus 15:26; 23:25; Psalm 103:2-3; 139:14; Proverbs 16:23-24; Isaiah 53:3-5; Matthew 4:23; 8:5-13; 8:5-13; 9:22,28-29; 10:8; Mark 11:23-24; Acts 3:6,16; 9:34; 14:8-10; Ephesians 1:18-23; 3:20; 1 Peter 2:24

_____

_____

_____

_____

_____

_____

My blood pressure is 120 over 80. My blood is flowing freely and cleansing my arteries of anything that doesn't belong there.

> Exodus 15:26; 23:25; Psalm 103:2-3; 139:14; Proverbs 16:23-24; Isaiah 53:3-5; Matthew 4:23; 8:5-13; 9:22,28-29; 10:8; Mark 11:23-24; John 14:12; Acts 3:6,16; 9:34; 14:8-10; Ephesians 1:20-23; 3:20; 1 Peter 2:24

_____

_____

_____

_____

_____

_____

_____

_____

I claim a healthy body. Health is my new birth right!

Psalm 103:2-3; Isaiah 53:3-5; Matthew 4:23; 8:5-13; 9:22,28-29; 10:8; John 10:10; 14:12; Acts 3:6,16; 9:34; 5:12-16; 14:8-10;28:8-9; 1 Corinthians 1:30; 5:7; 11:23-30; Ephesians 1:20-23; 3:20; 1 Peter 2:24

My God wants me to be HEALTHY. My God wants ME to be healthy. My health and well-being are a glory to my God, Who called me and saved me and bought me and HEALED me!

Exodus 15:26; Psalm 35:27; 103:2-5; 107:20-21; Isaiah 53:3-5; Matthew 4:23; 10:8; 14:14; Mark 8:22-25; Luke 18:35-43; John 14:12; Acts 3:1-8,16; 5:12-16; 9:34; 10:38; 14:8-10; 1 Corinthians 1:9; 6:20; Ephesians 1:2,20-23; 3:20; 2 Timothy 1:9; 1 Peter 2:24; 3 John 2

My Lord Jesus paid for my healing. I will honor him by gratefully receiving it.

Exodus 12:3,6-8,11; Psalm 105:37; Isaiah 53:3-5; Matthew 8:17; 10:8; 26:67; 27:26-35; Mark 14:65; 15:15-20,24-25; Luke 22:63-64; 23:33; Acts 3:6,16; 5:15-16; 9:34; 10:38; 14:8-10; 28:8-9; 1 Corinthians 5:7; 10:16; 11:23-30; Galatians 3:13; 1 Peter 1:18-19; 2:24

_____

_____

_____

_____

_____

_____

_____

You are my Father and I am Your child. With childlike faith I receive my healing from Your hand. Praise You!

Psalm 27:14; 73:28; 103:2-3; 107:20,21; Isaiah 40:31; 53:3-5; Matthew 4:23; 8:5-13; 9:22,28-29; 10:8; 11:5; 14:14; 15:31; Mark 5:25-34; 8:22-26; 9:23-24; Luke 18:35-42; John 9:1-7; 14:12; Acts 3:1-8,16; 5:15; 9:34; 14:8-10; Romans 8:15-16; Ephesians 1:2,19-23; 3:20; 1 Peter 2:24; 1 John 3:1-2; 5:14-15

_____

_____

_____

_____

_____

_____

CHAPTER 4

Living God's Love

Some of the declarations from previous chapters fall into the category of "loving" yourself; that is, seeing yourself as God sees you. Your healthy self-image and wholesome self-esteem are very important to Him. Why? Because His Son lovingly paid the ultimate price to redeem you, bringing you into the Father's family as an heir of God and joint heir with Christ.

This chapter begins with you affirming the love God has for you, which gives you every reason to properly love yourself. Then it encourages you to live intentionally and give God's love away, as an extension of His heart to others. What a privilege it is to represent the One Who showed us all what love looks like. What a powerful and LOVE-ly way to live!

God loves ME! He loves me right NOW! I get it!

Psalm 31:20-21; 103:13; 104:34; 105:3-4; Jeremiah 31:3; John 3:16; 14:21; 16:27; Romans 3:22-23; 5:8,17; 8:35-39; Ephesians 2:4; 2 Thessalonians 2:16; Titus 3:4-6; Hebrews 12:6; 1 Peter 5:7; 1 John 3:1-2; 4:8-19

What do you see as you read these scriptures? Do any more Bible verses come to mind? Any new affirmations?

_____

_____

_____

_____

_____

_____

My life is simple: I love God, I love myself and I love others... end of discussion.

Psalm 73:25-26; Matthew 22:37-40; Luke 10:29-37; John 12:43; 13:35; 14:15,31; 15:12; 17:26; 1 Corinthians 8:1-3; 13:1-13; 16:14; Ephesians 4:32; 5:1-2,28-29; Philippians 1:15-16; Colossians 3:14,19; 1 Timothy 1:5; 1 Peter 1:22; 4:8; 2 Peter 1:7; 1 John 3:18; 4:19-21; Jude 21

_____

_____

_____

_____

_____

_____

I am not a busy little robot for God... I'm in LOVE with God... I DELIGHT in God!

Deuteronomy 4:9; Psalm 1:2; 16:11; 27:4; 35:27-28; 37:4; 40:8; 73:25-26; 100:2; 103:1-2; 105:3-4; 111:2,10; 119:16,24; Jeremiah 9:23-24; Matthew 22:37-40; John 14:31; 1Corinthians 8:1-3; 13:1-3; Ephesians 6:10; Jude 21

_____

_____

_____

_____

_____

_____

_____

I love myself, so I treat my body lovingly. That's why I give it good food.

Leviticus 19:18; Proverbs 8:1,11: 19:8; 23:21; 25:28; Ecclesiastes 10:17; Matthew 19:19; 22:39; Romans 12:1; 13:9; 1 Corinthians 6:19-20; 9:25; 10:31; Galatians 5:14,22-25; Ephesians 1:18; 2:10; 5:29; Colossians 1:27; James 2:8; 2 Peter 1:6

_____

_____

_____

_____

_____

_____

_____

I love myself, so I treat my body lovingly. That's why I don't overeat.

Leviticus 19:18; Proverbs 8:1,11: 19:8; 23:21; 25:28; Ecclesiastes 10:17; Matthew 19:19; 22:39; Romans 12:1; 13:9; 1Corinthians 6:19-20; 9:25; 10:31; Galatians 5:14,22-25; Ephesians 1:18; 2:10; 5:29; Colossians 1:27; James 2:8; 2 Peter 1:6

_____

_____

_____

_____

_____

_____

_____

I love to give! I SHARE myself with others, but I refuse to COMPARE myself with others.

Psalm 133:1; Proverbs 14:30; 27:17; Luke 9:46-48; 10:29-37; 15:25-32; 18:9-14; John 13:13-17; 21:20-22; Romans 2:11; 12:3-16; 13:13-14; 14:1-13,19,22; 15:1-7; 1 Corinthians 3:3; 10:12; 13:4; 14:19; 1 Peter 4:8-10

_____

_____

_____

_____

_____

_____

_____

_____

I am kind, tenderhearted and forgiving of others because God is kind, tenderhearted and forgiving of me.

Proverbs 15:16-18; Matthew 18:21-22; Luke 6:36; 10:29-37; 15:25-32; Romans 2:4; 14:19; 1 Corinthians 13:4-7; Ephesians 2:7-8; 4:32; Colossians 3:13; Titus 3:3-6; James 5:11; 1 Peter 3:8-10; 4:8; 1 John 1:9; Jude 21

_____

_____

_____

_____

_____

_____

_____

_____

I will BUILD UP with my mouth. I will not tear down. My mouth will minister God's grace to others.

Psalms 34:13; Proverbs 11:11-13; 12:18,25; 13:3; 14:19; 15:1-2,4,16-18,30; 16:24; 17:27-28; 18:7-8,21; 20:19; 25:25; Matthew 12:34-35; Romans 13:13-14; 14:19; 1 Corinthians 3:3; 13:4-7; Ephesians 4:29; Colossians 3:8,12; Titus 3:2-9; 1 Peter 3:8-10; 4:10

_____

_____

_____

_____

_____

_____

_____

I was called to God's peace in one Body, along with my brothers and sisters. Furthermore, I am a peace maker.

Psalm 133:1; Proverbs 15:1-2,4,16-18; Matthew 5:9; John 17:21,26; Romans 5:1; 13:13-14; 14:19; 15:13; 1 Corinthians 3:3; 13:7; Galatians 6:1; Ephesians 2:14-18, 4:2-6,25-32; Philippians 4:2; Colossians 2:2; 3:10-15; James 3:16-18; 1 Peter 3:8-11; 5:5

_____

_____

_____

_____

_____

_____

I don't need to get my own way all the time ... I don't need to be right all the time ... I DO need to live God's love (all the time).

Proverbs 15:1-2,4,16-18; 21:2; John 13:13-17,34-35; Romans 13:13-14; 14:19; 15:5-6; 1 Corinthians 13:1-7; 14:1; Galatians 6:10; Ephesians 4:31-32; 5:1-2,21; Philippians 4:2; Colossians 3:8-14; 1 Thessalonians 3:12; 4:9-12; James 3:14-18; 1Peter 3:8-9; 1 John 3:11-19; 4:7-12

_____

_____

_____

_____

_____

_____

_____

_____

I choose the wisdom from above. I choose to live without envy and selfishness. I choose to live without partiality and hypocrisy. I choose peace.

Psalm 133:1; Proverbs 14:30; 15:16-18; John 14:12; Romans 12:18; 13:13-14; 14:19; 1 Corinthians 1:10; 3:3; 13:1-7; Ephesians 4:29-32; Colossians 3:12-15; 4:6; 1Thessalonians 4:9-12; James 3:13-18; 1 Peter 3:8-11; 1 John 4:19-21

_____

_____

_____

_____

_____

_____

_____

I'm so glad to be in the body of Christ with _____ !

Matthew 22:39; John 13:13-17,35; Romans 14:19; 15:1-7; 1 Corinthians 1:9-10; 3:3; 13:7; Ephesians 2:14-22; 3:9,17; 4:3-6,32; 5:19-21; Philippians 1:27; 2:1-5; 4:2-4; Colossians 3:12-15; 1 Peter 3:8-10; 4:8-10; 5:5; 1 John 4:20-21

_____

_____

_____

_____

_____

_____

_____

I do not use people, I use things. I LOVE people.

Deuteronomy 25:13-16; Proverbs 13:11; 16:8,18-20; 22:16; Ecclesiastes 5:10; Jeremiah 22:13; Malachi 3:5; Matthew 22:39; John 13:13-17; 1Corinthians 13:1-7; Ephesians 6:9; Philippians 2:1-5; Colossians 4:1; 1Thessalonians 4:6; 1 Timothy 5:21; James 2:6-9; 4:1-2; 5:4; 1 Peter 4:8; 1 John 2:15-17; 3:18

_____

_____

_____

_____

_____

_____

_____

NOTHING can keep me from loving. Nothing can make me UNloving.

Proverbs 15:17; Matthew 22:39; Luke 10:29-37; John 14:12; Romans 15:1-7; 1 Corinthians 13:7; 16:13-14; Galatians 6:10; Ephesians 5:1-2; 6:8; Philippians 1:9; 2:1-5; 1 Peter 4:8; 1 John 2:9-11; 3:16-18; 4:11-12,19-21

_____

_____

_____

_____

_____

_____

_____

Perfect love casts out all fear. I'm fearless because I'm a LOVER.

Luke 10:27-37; John 13:13-17; 14:12; Acts 4:13,29-31; 5:29,42; 28:31; 1 Corinthians 13:7; Ephesians 2:10; 6:19-20; Philippians 1:14; Hebrews 13:5-6; 1 Peter 3:15; 4:8; 1 John 2:6; 3:18-19; 4:7,17-21; Jude 20-21

_____

_____

_____

_____

_____

_____

_____

My name is _____ and Jesus is the Lord of my life. I walk in love, as he walked and I am as he is in this world!

Matthew 22:37-40; John 6:28-29; 13:13-17,35; 14:12; 15:9-17; 17:20-23,26; Romans 13:14; 15:1-7; Ephesians 4:32; 5:1-2; 6:24; Philippians 2:1-5; 2 Thessalonians 3:5; Hebrews 12:1-3; I John 2:6; 3:16-18; 4:16-21; 5:3,20

_____

_____

_____

_____

_____

_____

_____

_____

Help me to love like Christ. Teach me, Father how to love.

Matthew 9:35-38; 10:1,7-8; John 6:28-29; 13:13-17; 14:12; 15:9-17; 17:20-23,26; Acts 10:38; Romans 15:1-7; 16:25; Ephesians 2:10; 5:1-2; Philippians 1:9; 2:1-5,13; Colossians 3:9-17; 1Thessalonians 4:9-10; 2Thessalonians 3:5; Hebrews 12:1-3; 1 John 2:6; 3:16-18; 4:9-10; 5:3,20-21;

_____

_____

_____

_____

_____

_____

I cannot transform myself, Father... You know the person I can really be and only YOU can transform me... so I'll keep doing my job and I know that You'll do Yours.

1 Samuel 16:7; Psalm 16:7; 73:26; Matthew 3:11-12; John 3:6-7; 6:28-29,63; 15:1-5; 16:13-15; Romans 6:4; 7:18; 8:29; 12:2; 13:12-14; 16:25; 1 Corinthians 3:6-7; 14:12; 15:58; 2Corinthians 3:18; Galatians 5:16-23; Ephesians 1:17-19; 2:10; 4:22-24; Philippians 1:6,9; 2:12-13; 3:13-14; 4:1; Colossians 3:1-3,16; 1:27; 3:1-3,10-11; 2Thessalonians 3:5; Hebrews 12:6-11; 2 Peter 1:4-8; Jude 20-21

_____

_____

_____

_____

_____

_____

I will be authentic... off with the old nature and on with the new... it fits perfectly and I'm making a fashion statement!

Romans 6:3-11; 7:22-25; 8:6-8,13; 12:2-3,16-17; 13:13-14; 1Corinthians 2:8,12; 6:19-20; 13:1-7; 2Corinthians 2:14-15; 5:17; 8:21; Galatians 5:22-26; Ephesians 2:10; 4:22-24; Philippians 1:9; Colossians 1:27; 2:6; 3:3,9-11; 1Thessalonians 4:12; Titus 3:5; James 1:21-22; 2Peter 1:2-8

_____

_____

_____

_____

_____

_____

_____

_____

The love of God is IN me. GOD put it there. I CAN love.

Matthew 22:37-40; John 14:12; 17:26; Romans 5:5; Ephesians 2:10; 3:16-19; 5:1-2; Philippians 1:9; Colossians 1:27; 1Thessalonians 3:12; 2Thessalonians 3:5; 2Timothy 1:7; 1Peter 4:8; 2Peter 1:3-7; Jude 20-21; 1John 4:16-17

_____

_____

_____

_____

_____

_____

_____

51

Jesus could return TODAY. This could be my last day here. What kind of person do I want to be today?

Psalm 34:1; 118:24; John 14:12; Acts 1:8,11; 10:38; Romans 1:16; 13:12-14; 15:13; 1 Corinthians 12:7; 13:1-7; 14:12; 15:58; 2Corinthians 5:9,20; Ephesians 4:1,24; 5:1-2; 6:10; Philippians 2:5; 3:1,14; Colossians 3:23; 1 Timothy 6:19; 2 Timothy 2:1; 4:2,8; Hebrews 12:1; James 1:12; 1 Peter 1:22; 1 John 2:28; 3:3; 5:21; Jude 20-21

Note: For those who may be asking... yes, it is okay to use any or all of these declarations in one's own home, in relationship to one's spouse or other family members, but only those desiring positive results should do so.

_____

_____

_____

_____

_____

_____

_____

_____

_____

_____

_____

_____

_____

_____

_____

_____

_____

_____

CHAPTER 5

Living Prosperously

Does prosperity involve more than money? Absolutely. You've probably observed that anyone can have lots of money and still be miserable or sick. Prosperity must be understood from God's point of view, in order to avoid misconceptions.

Poverty, as well has certainly been a source of confusion for many. This chapter challenges you to discard a common, lingering myth: that being poor is somehow a virtuous way for Christians to live. You are invited to boldly embrace the prosperous state of mind that our heavenly Father wants all of His children to dwell in.

All believers receive the same wonderful spiritual benefits through Christ Jesus, because the Father does not have any favorite and "less favorite" children. We have all been highly favored! While certain obvious factors can and do affect a Christian's bank account in this life (e.g. ancestry, education, personal ambition, etc.), God's absolute will for all believers everywhere is prosperity and health. He desires to meet our material needs abundantly, and for us to enjoy His goodness, live thankfully and give Him the glory.

My name is _____ and Jesus is the Lord of my life. He redeemed me from the curse of the Old Testament Law and poverty! I think like he thought and I trust my Father in everything!

Deuteronomy 28:15-68; Psalm 84:11-12; Proverbs 3:5-6; 23:7; Mark 4:19; 11:22-24; John 10:10; 11:41-42; Romans 8:32; 10:9-11; 1 Corinthians 1:4-5; 2 Corinthians 8:9; 9:6-11; Galatians 3:13; 4:4-5; Ephesians 1:7; Philippians 2:5; 4:19; 1 Timothy 6:17; Hebrews 9:12-14; 1 Peter 5:6-7

What do you see as you read these scriptures? Do any more
Bible verses come to mind? Any new affirmations?

_____

_____

_____

_____

_____

I am RICH!... I will NEVER be poor again!... I have all that I need and more!

Genesis 13:2; 1Kings 3:7-14; 1Chronicles 4:10; 29:12,26; Psalm 4:8; 31:19-21,23; 35:27; 112:1-9; 119:14; Proverbs 3:16; 8:18-21; 10:4,22; 15:15-17; 17:1,22; 22:4; Ecclesiastes 5:18-19; Matthew 6:33; Acts 2:38-39; Romans 5:17; 8:32; 1Corinthians 1:3-5; 2Corinthians 8:9; 9:8; Ephesians 1:3,18; 2:7; 3:8; 3:16-20; Philippians 4:11-13,19; Colossians 1:12-13; 1:21-22,27; 2:2-3; 1Thessalonians 4:11-12; 1 Timothy 6:6-10,17; Hebrews 11:6; James 1:5; 2:23

_____

_____

_____

_____

I wait upon You, Father God, with expectation... expecting Your favor today... expecting You to bless me because You say that You will, and You never lie.

Numbers 23:19; Psalm 1:1-3; 25:1-5,14; 27:14; 34:15; 62:1-5; 68:19; 112:1-3,7-8; 119:90; Isaiah 40:31; Lamentations 3:22-25; Mark 9:23; 1Corinthians 1:9; Ephesians 3:20; Philippians 2:13; 4:19; Hebrews 10:23; 11:6; James 1:21-25; 4:6-7; 1 Peter 5:6-7; 3 John 2

_____

_____

_____

_____

_____

_____

_____

God's favor surrounds my life. He gives me all that I need. I AM RICH! He makes me rich, so that I can enrich others.

Joshua 1:8; 1Chronicles 29:12; Psalm 1:1-3; 23:1; 25:14; 34:8-10; 35:27; 37:3-5,25-26; 84:11-12; 92:12-15; Proverbs 3:9-10; 8:18-21; 11:25; 22:4; Isaiah 58:11; Jeremiah 17:7-8; Matthew 6:25-33; 1Corinthians 1:4-5; 2Corinthians 8:9; 9:6-8; Galatians 6:6; Philippians 4:19; Hebrews 11:6

_____

_____

_____

_____

_____

_____

_____

God blesses me, and I can bless others.

Psalm 1:1-3; 35:27; 37:3-5,25-26; 84:11-12; 92:12-15; 115:12-16; Proverbs 3:9,10; 8:18-21; 11:25; 28:20,25; Isaiah 58:11; Jeremiah 17:7-8; Matthew 6:25-33; 1Corinthians 1:4-5; 2Corinthians 8:9; 9:6-8; Galatians 6:6; Philippians 4:19; 1Timothy 6:17-18; Hebrews 11:6

_____

_____

_____

_____

_____

_____

_____

I refuse to think like a victim and I refuse to think like a mere survivor. I am a man/woman of means! My God withholds no good thing from me. I am blessed! I have it all!

Genesis 39:23; Numbers 14:8-9; 1Chronicles 29:11-12; Psalm 1:1-3; 23:1; 27:1,5; 34:8-10; 35:27; 37:3-5,25; 84:11-12; 92:12-15; Proverbs 3:5-10; 8:18-21; 22:4; 28:20,25; Isaiah 55:8-12; Joel 2:26-27; Matthew 6:25-33; Mark 11:23-24; Romans 5:17; 8:32; 1Corinthians 1:4-5; 2 Corinthians 8:9; 9:8; Ephesians 1:3-4; Philippians 4:19; Hebrews 11:6; 1John 5:14-15

_____

_____

_____

_____

_____

_____

I seek the BLESSER, not the blessing, and I know HE will bless me.

Leviticus 26:3-6; Joshua 1:8; 1Chronicles 29:11-12; Psalm 1:1-3; 34:4-10; 35:27; 37:3-5,11,25; 84:11-12; 92:12-15; 105:3-4; 112:1-3,7; 115:12-16; 119:2; 127:1; Proverbs 3:5-10; 8:18-21; Isaiah 26:3-9; 55:6; 58:11; Jeremiah 17:7-8; Malachi 3:10-12; Matthew 6:33; Galatians 6:7; Hebrews 11:6; James 1:5-7,17

_____

_____

_____

_____

_____

I don't care what the news media says about the economy. They aren't God. GOD is God! HE is my economic Advisor!

Genesis 39:23; Numbers 13:25-33; 14:8-9; 23:19; Deuteronomy 8:18; 1Chronicles 29:12; Psalm 1:1-3; 23:1; 25:14; 31:20; 34:8-10; 35:27; 37:3-5,11,25; 84:11-12; 92:12-15; 112:7; 115:12-16; Proverbs 3:5-10; 8:18-21; Isaiah 8:11-13; 55:8-12; 58:11; Jeremiah 17:7-8; Joel 2:26-27; Malachi 3:10-12; Matthew 6:24-34; Luke 6:38; 12:22-31; Romans 8:32; 2Corinthians 9:6-8; Philippians 4:19; 1Timothy 6:17; Hebrews 11:6; James 1:5-7; 1 John 5:14-15

_____

_____

_____

_____

_____

I refuse to have anxiety over money. God takes good care of me! He supplies all that I need!

Joshua 1:7-8; Psalm 1:1-3; 23:1; 25:14; 31:20; 34:8-10; 35:27; 37:3-5,25; 68:19; 84:11-12; 92:12; 115:12-16; 121:1-8; Proverbs 3:5-10; 8:18-21; 11:25; 23:4; 28:20-25; Isaiah 26:3; 55:8-12; Jeremiah 17:7-8; Joel 2:26-27; Matthew 6:25-34; Mark 11:24; Luke 12:22-31; Romans 8:32; 2Corinthians 9:8; Philippians 4:6,19; Hebrews 11:6; James 1:5-7,17; 1 John 5:14-15; 3 John 2

_____

_____

_____

_____

_____

_____

I am a man/woman of faith. I have faith because I know Who MY God is and what He can do!

Genesis 1:1; 39:23; Numbers 13:30, 23:19; Joshua 1:8-9; 1 Chronicles 29:11-12; Psalm 1:1-3; 25:14; 34:8-10; 35:27; 84:11-12; Proverbs 3:5-10; 8:18-21; 22:4; Isaiah 26:3; 55:8-12; 58:11; Jeremiah 17:7-8; Malachi 3:10-12; Matthew 6:24-34; Luke 6:38; 12:22-31; Romans 8:32; 2 Corinthians 9:8; Galatians 6:7; Philippians 4:19; Hebrews 11:6; James 1:5-7,17; 1 John 1:5

_____

_____

_____

_____

_____

_____

_____

My life is simple: I love God. He loves me. He takes care of me. End of discussion.

Psalm 1:1-3; 23:1; 25:14; 31:20; 34:8-10; 35:27; 37:1-7; 84:11-12; 92:12-15; 115:12-16; 121:1-8; Proverbs 3:5-10; 8:18-21; 11:25; 15:16-17; 22:4; 23:4; Jeremiah 17:7-8; Joel 2:26-27; Malachi 3:10-12; Matthew 6:24-34; Mark 4:19; Luke 10:27; Romans 8:32; 2 Corinthians 9:8; Galatians 6:7; Philippians 4:19; 1Timothy 6:17; Hebrews 11:6; 13:5-6; James 1:5-7; 1 Peter 5:7; 1 John 4:16-21; 5:14-15

_____

_____

_____

_____

_____

The Creator of the heavens and the Earth is my Partner in life!

Genesis 1:1; Deuteronomy 8:18; Joshua 1:8; 1Chronicles 29:11-12; Psalm 1:1-3; 23:1; 25:14; 34:9; 35:27; 37:1-7; 84:11-12; 92:12-15; 105:3-5; 115:12-16; Proverbs 3:5-10; 8:18-21; 22:4; Ecclesiastes 5:19; Isaiah 58:11; Jeremiah 17:7,8; Joel 2:26-27; Malachi 3:10-12; Matthew 6:31-33; Romans 5:17; 8:32; 2 Corinthians 9:8; Galatians 6:7; Philippians 4:19; 1Timothy 4:8; 6:17; Hebrews 11:6; 13:5-6; James 1:5-7,17; 1 John 4:16-21; 5:14-15

_____

_____

_____

_____

_____

(as you tithe) I am doing this to honor YOU. Everything I have comes from YOU. My job is not my source... YOU are my Source!

Deuteronomy 8:18; 1 Chronicles 29:11,12; Psalm 1:1-3; 23:1; 34:9; 35:27; 37:3-5,25,34; 50:10; 84:11-12; 115:12-16; Proverbs 3:5-10; 8:18-21; Isaiah 58:11; Jeremiah 17:7-8; Joel 2:26-27; Malachi 3:10-12; Matthew 6:33; Romans 8:32; 1 Corinthians 1:4-5; 2 Corinthians 9:8; Galatians 6:6-7; Philippians 4:19; 1Timothy 6:17; Hebrews 11:6; 13:5-6; James 1:5-7,17

_____

_____

_____

_____

_____

_____

(as you tithe) I LOVE to GIVE! Thank-you, Father for the chance to give!

1 Chronicles 29:9; Psalm 37:26; 105:3-4; Proverbs 3:9-10,27; 11:24-25; 21:26; 22:9; 28:27; Isaiah 58:6-11; Malachi 3:10-12; Matthew 6:1-4; Mark 12:41-44; Luke 6:38; Acts 4:34-35; 20:35: 1 Corinthians 16:2; 2 Corinthians 9:6-8; Galatians 6:6-7; Philippians 4:15-19; 1 Timothy 6:17-18; James 2:15-16

_____

_____

_____

_____

_____

_____

_____

Everything I "own" is for God's glory. That's why I take good care of my stuff and spend my money wisely.

Deuteronomy 8:10-18; Psalm 8:4-8; 50:10-11; 89:11; 112:5; 24:1; Proverbs 6:5-6; 10:21; 15:16-17; 17:18; 21:20; 22:7,26-27; 24:3-4; Matthew 25:14-39; Luke 16:1-10; 1 Corinthians 4:2; 6:19-20; Ephesians 5:15-17; Colossians 3:23; 1 Timothy 6:17-18; 2 Timothy 6:6-11

_____

_____

_____

_____

_____

_____

_____

God has blessed me and I'm a good steward.

Deuteronomy 8:10-18; Psalm 8:4-8; 50:10-11; 89:11; 112:5; 24:1; Proverbs 6:5-6; 10:21; 15:16-17; 17:18; 21:20; 22:7,26-27; 24:3-4; Matthew 25:14-39; Luke 16:1-10; 1 Corinthians 4:2; 6:19-20; Ephesians 5:15-17; Colossians 3:23; 1 Timothy 6:17-18; 2 Timothy 6:6-11

_____

_____

_____

_____

_____

_____

_____

 CHAPTER 6

Personal Goals

As members of the Body of Christ we are all on a glorious path together, our destination being eternity with God! The blessed hope we have of the return of God's Son and our gathering together up to him encourages and comforts us as no other upcoming event possibly can. In the meantime, as we live in this world and patiently wait for that day, we look to God to illuminate our individual paths. We need His direction in our lives, His guidance, His inspiration, His open doors.

Has God put any specific desires on your heart that would enable you to use your talents and abilities? What would you like to accomplish with His help? Start your own business? Write a book? Complete your education? Get out of debt? Do full time ministry work? You are a unique individual with much to offer, and you and God can make it happen, for His glory.

I acknowledge You, Father. I know that You are directing my paths.

> Genesis 39:23; Psalm 27:5; 35:27; 73:26; 119:105; 146:2; 147:11; Proverbs 2:8; 3:5-6; 4:18; 9:10; 16:1-3,9; 18:12; 22:4; Isaiah 48:17; 57:15; 66:2; Micah 6:8; Mark 12:30; Philippians 2:13; Hebrews 11:6; 1 Peter 5:6-7;
>
> *What do you see as you read these scriptures? Do any more Bible verses come to mind? Any new affirmations?*

_____

_____

_____

_____

_____

You have known me all my life, from the moment I was conceived. You HAVE guided me and I believe that You ARE guiding me at THIS very moment of my life. I believe that you are opening the doors for me and putting me in the right place at the right time.

> Genesis 39:3-4,21-23; Deuteronomy 8:18-19; 1 Chronicles 4:9-10; Psalm 1:1-3; 25:14; 27:5; 35:27; 37:4-5; 112:1-3; 139:1-24; Proverbs 2:8; 3:5-6; 4:18; 16:1-3,9; 28:25-26; Isaiah 48:17; 57:15; 66:2; Jeremiah 17:7-8; Mark 11:24; Acts 10:17-20,30-33,44; 1 Timothy 6:17; Hebrews 11:6; James 1:5; 1 Peter 5:6-7

_____

_____

_____

_____

_____

God's favor surrounds my life... it moves mountains for me... it opens doors for me... it causes people to want to help me.

Genesis 39:3-4,21-23; Leviticus 26:9; Deuteronomy 8:18; 31:6; 1 Samuel 2:26; 1 Chronicles 4:9-10; Ezra 7:27-28; Psalm 1:1-3; 5:12; 25:14; 27:5,14; 35:27; 84:11; 103:4-5; 112:1-3; Proverbs 3:5-6; 4:18; 10:22; 16:1-3,9; 22:4; 28:20,25; Isaiah 48:17; Jeremiah 17:7-8; 29:11; Mark 11:23-24; Romans 5:17; 1 Corinthians 1:4; 2 Corinthians 9:8; Ephesians 3:20; 2 Peter 3:18

_____

_____

_____

_____

_____

_____

Father, here I am. Please help me to live to my full potential in this life as Your child, for Your glory.

Psalm 1:1-3; 35:27; 37:3-5; Proverbs 3:5-6; 4:18; 10:22; 13:4; 16:1-3,9; 18:12; 28:20,25-26; Ecclesiastes 9:10; Isaiah 48:17; Jeremiah 9:23-24; 17:7-8; Micah 6:8; Matthew 6:33; Mark 12:30; Luke 6:38; Romans 5:17; 1 Corinthians 1:4-5; 6:19-20; 16:13; Ephesians 3:20; Philippians 2:13; Colossians 3:23; 2 Thessalonians 1:3; 1Timothy 4:7-8; 6:17; James 1:5,21-25; 1 Peter 5:5-7

_____

_____

_____

_____

_____

_____

I will be victorious in this situation. God will bring me through, victoriously.

Deuteronomy 31:6; 1 Samuel 17:40-54; 2 Kings 6:15-23; 1 Chronicles 4:9-10; Job 42:10-17; Psalm 1:1-3; 27:5,14; 31:1-24; 46:1-2,10-11; 62:1-2,5-8; 73:25-26; 91:2; 94:17-19; 105:37-45; 107:28-31; 112:7-8; 124:8; 138:7-8; 145:18; Proverbs 3:5-6; Isaiah 41:10,13; Romans 8:37; 1 Corinthians 10:13; 2 Corinthians 1:10; 2:14; Colossians 1:11; Hebrews 4:16; James 1:2-8,12-13; 4:10; 1 Peter 5:10

_____

_____

_____

_____

_____

_____

YOU gave me the inspiration for this and YOU are for me... I will not quit!

Deuteronomy 8:18; Psalm 1:1-3; 16:7; 27:14; 35:27; Proverbs 3:5-6,26; 16:1-3,9; 18:12; 21:5; 27:14; 28:20; Isaiah 48:17-18; Jeremiah 17:7-8: Mark 11:24; Romans 8:31-39; Hebrews 10:35; 11:6; James 1:5-8

_____

_____

_____

_____

_____

_____

NOTHING is impossible with God!

Genesis 15:1-7; 18:14; Deuteronomy 8:18; 10:14; 31:6; 1 Chronicles 4:9-10; Psalm 105:5; 115:3; 135:6; Isaiah 40:28-31; 46:9-10; 48:17; Jeremiah 32:27; 51:15; Matthew 7:7,11; 19:26; Mark 10:27; 11:23-24; Luke 1:37; John 11:22-23,41-44; Romans 4:19-21; Ephesians 3:20

_____

_____

_____

_____

_____

_____

_____

If I keep moving, I'll get there, with God's help! If I don't, I won't.

Deuteronomy 31:6; 1 Chronicles 4:9-10; Psalm 27:14; Proverbs 3:5-6,26; 4:18; 6:6-11; 10:4; 13:4; 16:1-3,9; 21:5; 28:19-20; Ecclesiastes 5:19; Isaiah 40:31; 48:17-18; 1 Corinthians 4:2; 16:13; Philippians 2:13; Hebrews 10:36

_____

_____

_____

_____

_____

_____

_____

I refuse to think small. I have a HUGE God!

Deuteronomy 4:7; 8:18; 10:14; 1 Chronicles 4:9-10; Psalm
105:5; 135:6; Proverbs 3:5-6,26; 15:3; Isaiah 40:12-18; 46:9-10;
66:1; Jeremiah 9:23-24; 17:7-8; 48:17-18; 51:15; Mark 11:23-24;
Ephesians 3:20; Hebrews 11:6; James 1:5-8

_____

_____

_____

_____

_____

_____

Father God, this is my vision for _____. I believe
it is entirely possible, with Your help and I believe you are
working with me.

Deuteronomy 8:18; 31:6; 1 Chronicles 4:9-10; Psalm 1:1-3; 32:8;
35:27; 127:1-2; Proverbs 3:5-6; 4:18; 16:1-3,9; 18:12; 21:5; Isaiah
40:31; 48:17-18; Jeremiah 17:7-8; Mark 9:23; Philippians 2:13;
James 1:5-8; 1 Peter 5:6; 1 John 5:14

_____

_____

_____

_____

_____

_____

_____

God, the Creator of the heavens and the Earth is my Partner in life!

> Deuteronomy 8:18; 31:6; Psalm 1:1-3; 25:14; 27:5; 32:8; 35:27; 112:1; 127:1-2; 147:11; Proverbs 3:5-6,26; 4:18; 16:1-3,9; 22:4; Ecclesiastes 5:19; 12:1,13-14; Isaiah 40:31; 46:9-10; 48:17; 66:1,2; Jeremiah 9:23-24; 17:7-8; 48:17,18; 51:15; Micah 6:8; Luke 12:7; 16:13; Hebrews 11:6; 1 Corinthians 1:3-5; 1 John 5:14-15,20-21

_____

_____

_____

_____

_____

_____

God is guiding my steps. He has promised to do so. I AM walking with God. He has never failed me and He won't fail me now.

> Genesis 39:23; Deuteronomy 8:18; 31:6; Psalm 1:1-3; 25:14; 27:5,14; 32:8; 35:27; 73:25-26; 105:3-5; Proverbs 2:8; 3:5-6,26; 4:18; 15:3; 16:1-3,9; 18:12; Ecclesiastes 12:1,13-14; Isaiah 40:31; 48:17-18; Jeremiah 9:23-24; 17:7-8; Micah 6:8; Hebrews 10:35-36; 11:6; 13:6; James 1:2-8; 1 John 1:5-9

_____

_____

_____

_____

_____

_____

_____

God made EVERYTHING and God knows EVERYTHING... Gee, He probably even knows what I should do with my life!

Deuteronomy 8:18; 10:14; Psalm 1:1-3; 32:8; 33:6; 35:27; Proverbs 3:5-6,19,26; 15:3; 16:1-3,9; Ecclesiastes 9:10; 12:1,13-14; Isaiah 40:14; 48:17; Jeremiah 9:23-24; 17:7; 48:17-18; 51:15-19; Luke 12:7; Romans 12:1-8; Philippians 2:13; Colossians 3:23; 1 Timothy 4:7-8; James 1:5-8; 1 John 1:5

_____

_____

_____

_____

_____

_____

_____

_____

_____

_____

_____

_____

_____

_____

_____

_____

_____

_____

_____

_____

_____

Conclusion

Regardless of their places in His story (history), God's people have always lived amidst challenges in the world, as well as in their personal lives. Thankfully they have also heard His loving assurances of... *I am with you... I will help you... don't be afraid... etc.*

As we open the Bible today in the 21st century our eyes behold timeless truths woven throughout its pages by divine design, and our hearts, too become well-assured and illuminated. Realities such as the Author's unchanging nature, His concern for our well-being, His ability to restore shattered lives, His faithfulness to perform His Word, to name a few. God has spoken, and is speaking right now, through His written Word.

So much in our everyday lives is affected by words. The daily decision to say positive, loving things to ourselves and to others is so basic, and much of the joy of living can be lost when we don't. Let's face it, we are always thinking or saying *something*, every waking moment of our lives. Why not endeavor to think like God thinks? Why not say things that He would agree with?

Your deliberate verbal confessions are indeed powerful and the right ones can help you become the person you want to be. In closing, I'd like to emphasize however that there is really no substitute for spending time in God's Word; simply reading it, enjoying it, meditating on it, and allowing its message to permeate your heart.

Have you ever read the entire Bible, from cover to cover? If not, I would like to encourage you to make this a personal project. I also highly recommend memorizing some scriptures as you do, storing them in your personal arsenal, and "firing" them as needed. You can declare, just as Jesus did ... *it is written...* during moments of uncertainty, anxiety, anger, fear, envy, or anything else negative that knocks at your door.

Can Bible verses be spoken or sung during happy and carefree moments as well? Absolutely. This is one simple means of giving God the recognition and praise that He wants and that He alone deserves. He is, after all, the reason for everything… for you, for me, the universe, and life itself. What a privilege it is to know Him and to walk in agreement with Him. What greater adventure could any man or woman possibly desire?

Let's all say it together:

To GOD be the glory! GREAT things He has done!

CPSIA information can be obtained at www.ICGtesting.com
Printed in the USA
BVOW07s1955081113

335843BV00001B/16/P

9 781490 804071